OOPS! I DROPPED MY SUPER POWERS

Live a Life that Leaves a Legacy: No Super Powers Required

Mary Watson-Burton

Apprise Solutions Pty Ltd

The characters and events portrayed in this book are fictitious. Any similarity to real persons, living or dead, is coincidental and not intended by the author.

ISBN-13: 978-0-6484504-1-2

Cover design by: Art Painter
Library of Congress Control Number: 2018675309
Printed in the United States of America

For My Daughters

CONTENTS

A GUIDE TO RECLAIMING YOUR LEGACY

★ ★ ★

"You pay for your life with the footsteps you leave behind."
Who Pays the Ferryman? BBC, 1977

THE LEGACY QUESTION

What do I want to be remembered for? Who do I want to be remembered as?

Two questions. That's it.

Hold them in your mind for a moment and notice what they stir.

These are the questions at the heart of this book. Not because they are complicated — they are almost disarmingly simple — but because they are the right questions. They are the questions that shift the paradigm of how you make decisions, how you spend your time, how you show up in your own life.

This book is built on these two questions. Together they are what I call the Legacy Question. And from the moment they are genuinely asked — not skimmed over, but asked and held — everything can begin to change.

The Legacy Question is not about death. It is about life — specifically, your life, right now, and the kind of person you want to be in it. It is a lens through which daily choices become clearer. It is a compass. And once you start using it, you will find you cannot put it down.

WHAT THIS BOOK IS

Did you ever feel like Wonder Woman through your twenties, thirties, and into your forties? The time when you power through following a sleepless night, make it to the 7.30am meeting, compete in the workplace to have your voice heard and do not drop dead by 6pm. The demands of living life are often high and women seem to have an unending capacity to multi-task.

Living life as if we are Wonder Woman, though, is not all it's cracked up to be. Sometimes we crack. And at some stages of life it feels like we have dropped our Super Powers entirely.

If that is where you are — or where you have been — this book is for you.

This book is for you if you are wondering what's next. If you want to reconnect with your authentic self. If you want to know where your real motivation comes from. If you want to stop being everything to everyone else and instead simply be yourself — present, purposeful, alive.

This book is also for you if you want to challenge your thinking and shift your paradigm.

At the centre of this book is a concept I call the Legacy Space — the place where your Being and your Doing overlap. Where you are in the zone, where your energy levels are up, where your Super Powers might now be hiding. It is the intersection of who you are with what you do. When you discover how to connect with it, you will uncover a power you always had.

All of us are here as a result of the legacy of those who have come before us — a direct descendant, or as part of a culture, a society, a tribe. The journey I invite you on is to challenge your personal status quo, embrace the discomfort that comes with personal examination, and use the time you have to live life from your legacy space and leave a legacy for others.

You will leave a legacy. The only question is whether it will be accidental or intentional.

PART ONE

THE PROBLEM

Why We Lose Our Superpowers — And What Balance Has to Do With It

WHY WE LOSE OUR SUPERPOWERS

There comes a moment — often in your forties or fifties, though it can arrive earlier or later — when the noise stops and a question rises in the silence: Who am I now?

It might arrive in the gap that follows raising a family, when the daily demands that once filled every hour suddenly ease and you realise you have been so busy doing that you have lost track of your being. It might come with a career change, a relationship ending, a health scare, or the quiet arrival of a significant birthday. It might not arrive with any particular drama at all — just a creeping sense that the self you once knew has slipped out of reach.

This feeling — the sense of having dropped your Super Powers — is not weakness. It is a signal. Something meaningful is asking for your attention.

The women who navigate this crossroads most effectively, who emerge more energised and purposeful on the other side, share something in common: they ask themselves a different question. Not what should I be doing? but who do I want to be remembered as?

That shift — from doing to being, from busyness to legacy — is the entire journey of this book.

THE DEMANDS WE CARRY

Women in midlife are often described as the "sandwich generation" — caught between the needs of children (or grandchildren) and ageing parents, between career demands and domestic ones, between what the world expects and what their own hearts are asking for. The mental load carried by this generation is extraordinary. The emotional labour is rarely acknowledged.

There may never have been a more significant time for women to remain engaged, to forge ahead, and to challenge the status quo. And yet the tools typically offered — goal-setting frameworks, productivity systems, the relentless pressure toward "balance" — often serve to increase the load rather than lighten it.

This book offers something different. Not a system. Not a formula. A question. And from that question, a framework that is entirely yours.

* * *

BALANCE IS A MYTH

Before we go any further, let's clear something up.

Balance is a myth.

There. It is said. And the relief you may feel in reading it is entirely appropriate.

Not because balance is wrong as an aspiration, but because the way it is typically promoted — as a constant, achievable state where all parts of life are simultaneously honoured in equal measure — is a fiction. A seductive, exhausting, guilt-inducing fiction.

Think about every achievement you know of that required real commitment. The 10,000 hours of practice required to master a skill. The intense focus of building a business from scratch. The sacrifice of an athlete in training. The total absorption of a writer or artist in their work. Every single one of these required imbalance — a deliberate, chosen tilting of focus toward what mattered most.

Balance is not what creates extraordinary things. Focus does. Passion does. The willingness to put more into one area of life, for a season, knowing other areas will wait.

WHAT BALANCE ACTUALLY COSTS WOMEN

The idea of balance has a particular hold on women's lives, and it is worth examining what it costs. The pressure to balance career and family, to balance ambition and relatability, to balance self-care and self-sacrifice, has often functioned as a mechanism to keep women's full power in check. If a woman is always dividing her attention equally, she is never fully deploying it anywhere.

The argument for structural gender balance — in the workplace, on boards, in government — is a different conversation entirely. It is a systemic issue and one that genuinely matters. But the myth of personal balance — the idea that each individual woman must divide herself equally among all her roles at all times — is a construct that serves no one, least of all her.

Tipping the scales toward what matters most is not a failure. It might be the most honest and courageous thing you do.

WHAT TO DO INSTEAD

Living from your Legacy Space — which we will explore in depth in Part Three — will provide clarity and focus. But it will mean that some parts of your life will appear temporarily unbalanced. This is not something to be ashamed of. It is something to understand and own.

Why does Wonder Woman have an alter ego? It is pretty simple, really. When Diana has to focus on saving the day, she spins in a circle, zaps on her best jewellery, and directs all her attention to the task at hand. Inwardly she is exactly the same person she was a moment before — same values, same character — but outwardly she looks different. Because she is differently focused.

Balance could be the myth holding you back from living a life that leaves a legacy. Living from your legacy will provide you with clarity and focus, and may indeed mean some parts of your life appear unbalanced — temporarily. Your true power lies in the quiet space where Being and Doing intersect.

Let balance go.

PART TWO

WHY LEGACY MATTERS

Accidental and Intentional — and Everything In Between

YOU WILL LEAVE A LEGACY

We all leave a legacy — accidental or intentional.

You will leave a legacy. You will leave an impact. If you have any doubt about this, pause for a moment and consider a teacher who shifted your thinking. A friend you lost touch with many years ago who sat with you when you wanted to cry. A stranger who introduced you to an idea that changed how you saw the world. Perhaps they gave you a new perspective, an insight, a richness you would not otherwise have had. This is how a legacy unfolds — moment by moment, spanning a lifetime.

None of us navigate life without the grief of losing someone we loved. In the gap between loss and continuing living, in the days of mourning, we cast our thoughts back through the life of the person we have lost and, in doing so, we examine their legacy. What did they mean? What did they leave? What of them continues?

That process — the one we instinctively do for others — is the one this book invites you to do for yourself, while you are still here to shape the answer.

A legacy can be small. It can be wide. It can be felt through generations, through culture, through a single life forever changed by an encounter with yours. It can be traumatic or uplifting, accidental or intentional. But it is always real.

The Legacy Question exists to help you make yours intentional.

Intentional vs. Accidental Legacy

Every legacy falls somewhere on a spectrum between accidental and intentional. Understanding where yours currently sits is the first step toward choosing where you want it to go.

An intentional legacy is one shaped by conscious choice. It is built by people who have asked themselves what matters to them, and then arranged their time, energy, and effort accordingly. We all know of people who, following a significant event — a loss, a diagnosis, a shift in circumstance — started a charity, became a leader, fought for a cause. They experienced a trigger event, decided to create change, and in doing so created a narrative that would influence others.

Intentional legacies are also created without dramatic triggers. Every day, people from all walks of life are engaging their talents and passion in areas of science, art, engineering, politics, community, and family — living from a space they enjoy, building a story of who they will be remembered as.

An accidental legacy is one left by default — the unexamined patterns we pass on, the values we model without choosing them, the behaviours that ripple forward through time without our awareness or intention. An accidental legacy is not necessarily negative, but it is unconscious. And unconscious legacies, as we will see, can carry considerable weight.

★ ★ ★

OOPS, I LEFT A LEGACY!

What we do now echoes in eternity.

Marcus Aurelius

Legacy matters. Your legacy matters. You may not be aware how important it is — or how silently and invisibly a legacy can shape a life. To understand this at its most profound, consider the story of Annie.

ANNIE'S STORY

Annie was buried on 8 February, 1888. Two days later, following reports from neighbours that there had been fighting in the home, police exhumed Annie's body. An autopsy revealed that Annie's brain was in a semi-fluid condition — possibly the result of violence.

A coroner's inquest followed a week later, the proceedings fully detailed in a New Zealand newspaper, The Star. Remarkably, the inquest heard reports from two of Annie's daughters: Elizabeth, fourteen, and Hannah, thirteen. Five neighbours provided information to the inquest, highlighting a strained family life punctuated by bouts of violence, precipitated by alcohol. Combined, their testimonies revealed the life of a woman living in fear and turmoil, stoically holding together her family, marriage, and reputation in the community.

Until recently the story of Annie and the questionable circumstances around her death had been lost to future generations. The discovery of the 1888 newspaper unveiled a secret kept hidden in a vain attempt to protect and pretend. A resulting failure to examine the actions of Annie's husband enabled a pattern of domestic abuse and fractured families to develop over the next three generations.

Annie and her husband, John, had emigrated from England in the early 1880s. John arrived in 1880 and three of their elder children followed in 1884. Annie undertook the arduous ship journey with only the youngest of their children in 1886. She was to die just two years later, at forty years old, leaving behind seven children, including a baby of just eighteen months.

According to neighbours who testified at the inquest, Annie was a sober, hard-working woman, friendly and a good mother to her children. They had provided refuge to Annie and the children following altercations with John, and stated that while John was usually pleasant enough, he was "always on at his wife" and "it was a pity that he drank." They believed Annie was desperate to leave, but returned home after each violent episode on John's promise that he would stop drinking.

Annie's daughters provided specific testimony to the events that occurred three days prior to her death. John had arrived home drunk and demanded his food before verbally abusing Annie. He struck her, causing a mark near her ear. He hit her again, causing her nose to bleed. He then threatened her with a penknife. Elizabeth stated that although her father often struck her mother, it was "always with an open hand."

The family took refuge with a neighbour for the night, and the following day Annie resumed her dressmaking work. In the afternoon she complained of feeling unwell — vague, dizzy, and sick to her stomach — and went to her bed. Annie seldom complained of her mistreatment.

The physician who conducted the autopsy testified that he had found the brain in an extremely unusual condition — semi-fluid and foetid — a condition not associated with British Cholera, the cause of death on Annie's official death certificate. He concluded that Annie's death was a result of the condition of the brain, but could not state that this condition was a direct result of violence.

Following this, the coroner advised the jury that no evidence presented supported any finding other than the medical testimony. The jury judged in agreement. John was not charged, nor admonished for his behaviour towards his wife.

Annie's daughters would go on to live with the weight of what they had witnessed. The pattern John had modelled — of power and violence in the home — did not end with Annie's death. It rippled forward, through generations, in the way unexamined legacies tend to do: silently, invisibly, and with considerable force.

WHAT ANNIE TELLS US

Annie never would have wanted to leave a legacy of the tolerance of abuse. It is reasonable to imagine she had other plans — a plan to leave, to grow her dress-making business, to enjoy her life. She was a skilled, sociable, hard-working woman doing her best in an era that gave her little power and fewer options. She was living in a New Zealand where women were, at that very moment, standing up and signing petitions demanding the right to vote. Meanwhile, Annie, and no doubt many others, kept their abuse secret.

What Annie's story makes visible is this: every one of us is already leaving a legacy. The only question is whether it is the legacy we would choose.

According to findings in the report Against the Odds: How Women Survive Domestic Violence (Keys Young, 1998), women living in violent situations are unlikely to seek outside support due to fear, isolation, lack of support, and shame. An Australian Bureau of Statistics survey, Women's Safety Australia (1996), found that only 4.5% of women who were physically assaulted contacted a crisis organisation — while as many as 58% discussed their situation with a friend or neighbour.

The health of our society, the level of safety, quality of relationships, and peace of mind we experience as a community is something each of us, consciously or not, contributes to. Awareness and examination of these fundamentals can enable us to respond to others, extend our support, act with integrity, and become more compassionate. Sharing Annie's story — documented in the public record, named in a newspaper, witnessed by her daughters and her neighbours — may provide some small chance for a shift in the life of a woman you know, or in your own future generations. That is itself an intentional legacy.

* * *

INTERGENERATIONAL TRAUMA

Intergenerational trauma is a real and potent legacy, bearing a profound effect on the lives of people we know and love. Our lives are often shaped by the unconscious beliefs and experiences of previous generations — and are often part of a family pattern of behaviour, or a gap in the traditions of families when those families have been torn apart.

This type of intergenerational trauma exists for Aboriginal populations of Australia and is spoken of by Native American tribes; we are now beginning to understand the transmission and impact of such trauma on persons displaced by war, genocide, and the Holocaust.

For a beautifully told story and in-depth insight into the profound impact of intergenerational trauma, seek out Leah Warshawski's TEDx Twin Falls talk, How Do You Cope with the Trauma You Didn't Experience. Leah calmly and methodically steps her audience through the personal story of her grandmother Sonja, a survivor of the Holocaust. Despite a family life Leah describes as "perfect," she could feel a "looming drama." Eventually a family journey and the questions Leah raised broke the emotional wall, followed by Leah investing her time in creating a documentary about Sonja. It is a remarkable, beautifully told insight into the real lived experience of intergenerational trauma.

The history of the Herero people of Namibia provides another striking example. Between 24,000 and 100,000 people were driven to death through dehydration and starvation following a rebellion in 1904 — an attempted genocide whose effects continue to reverberate through the generations of Herero descendants today.

> "Although this genocide happened a hundred and something years ago, it feels as if it were yesterday. No matter how old a wound is, once you prop it open, it becomes just as painful." — Mekahako Komomungondo, speaking of visiting the remains of her ancestors

This is the nature of intergenerational trauma — a wound that passes through generations without a name, until someone gives it one.

"Aren't we all surviving something or someone?" asks Leah Warshawski. "Aren't we all trying to deal with some sort of trauma we didn't experience on our own? Because we can't choose our parents, we can't choose our grandparents; we don't decide what happens to us along the way."

If we are all surviving something or someone, it is a clear indication that legacy is never built alone.

★ ★ ★

EPIGENETICS

Science is providing additional insights into how trauma is transmitted through generations — and the news is both challenging and hopeful.

The field is called epigenetics, and it is opening the door to a real understanding of how trauma manifests at a biological as well as a social level.

A combined study led by researchers at the EMBL-CRG Systems Biology Unit and the Joseph Carreras Leukaemia Research Institute found that the impact of environmental change can be passed on in genes for many generations. "We discovered this phenomenon by chance," noted the lead researcher, "but it shows that it's certainly possible to transmit information about the environment down the generations."

A Nature Neuroscience study reported by the BBC found evidence of "transgenerational epigenetic inheritance" — in which the environment can affect an individual's genetics, which can in turn be passed on. Professor Marcus Pembrey from University College London described the findings as "highly relevant to phobias, anxiety, and post-traumatic stress disorders," and as providing "compelling evidence that a form of memory can be passed between generations."

The key insight from all of this is not fatalistic — it is empowering. Trauma is transmitted. But so is healing. Your legacy includes both the patterns you have inherited and the patterns you choose to break. An intentional legacy, lived from your Legacy Space, is itself an act of healing — for yourself, and for those who come after you.

Trauma occurring to one can and does affect many. But so does courage. So does the choice to examine what has been left unexamined, to name what has been kept secret, and to begin again.

Now we know how much a legacy matters — let's find some answers of our own.

PART THREE

YOUR LEGACY FRAMEWORK

Values, Exercises, and Finding Your Legacy Space

Oops! I Dropped My Super Powers

> "Don't let your special character and values, the secret that you know and no one else does — the truth — don't let that get swallowed up by the great chewing complacency."
>
> Aesop

Of course there are women out there who juggle life and never seem to drop anything. But equally, there are women who have discovered that juggling cannot go on forever. At some point the balls drop. The Super Powers end up on the floor.

So what is happening internally when we feel our Super Powers have forsaken us? What is going on when change happens — when we have been thumping along the supersonic highway of life and suddenly we stop and begin asking the big questions: Who am I now? Why am I here?

There could be a myriad of circumstances: illness, divorce, death, family responsibilities, children leaving home, redundancy. Equally, it could be a change of house or country, a new grandchild, a wedding, a relationship beginning or ending. Any significant shift in what we are doing creates space where we must ask who we are being.

What you are experiencing when you find yourself wondering what shifted is a shift in values. It can feel like a chasm has opened up and you are staring into an abyss.

Here is a way to understand it:

Imagine for a moment you are sitting in a room reading a book — you are possibly experiencing an expression of a value you hold of curiosity or learning. Suddenly the room begins to shake. Your awareness moves from the pages to your wider environment. The room shakes more and you know you are in an earthquake. Your values shift automatically from curiosity to survival and you take action. The earthquake calms. You begin to shift back — probably not straight to the book, but to your phone to check on friends. Caring is a value too.

This is values in action: constantly shifting, responding, prioritising. Life events — the ending of a marriage, the departure of a last child, a significant health event — shake your inner landscape and shift your values priorities.

The good news is this: the values themselves never leave. They are yours. They are you. It is just a matter of reconnecting with them and choosing, intentionally, which ones to lead with.

UNDERSTANDING THE LEGACY SPACE

Your true power lives in the quiet space where Being and Doing intersect.

When you are operating from the Legacy Space, you find an effortless supply of inspiration and energy. Time passes without your noticing it. You feel most like yourself. This is the zone, the flow state — and it is not random. It is available to you every time you align what you value with what you do.

The Legacy Space can be felt in these moments: when your children were young and you found endless energy to advocate for and protect them. When caring for a loved one who was ill or struggling, you found strength of spirit and a capacity to organise you did not know you had. When drawn to a cause or a project that made you feel completely alive.

Those moments were not accidents. They were you, living from your Legacy Space.

Your challenge now is to discover how to connect with it again and again — not by accident, but by choice.

EXERCISE ONE: Identify Your Values

What follows is the core exercise of this book. It is simple. It is not a test. There is no right or wrong answer. It is an act of honest inquiry — and it is the foundation of everything that comes next.

STEP 1 — Grab a piece of paper and write down in list form the numbers 1 through to 13.

STEP 2 — While thinking about your life and what is most important to you right now, write one word next to each number. Keep going until all 13 are filled. These are examples only — use your own words: Family, Friends, Learning, Love, Kindness, Spirituality, Forgiveness, Discovery, Courage, Connection, Finance/Security, Strength, Wellbeing.

STEP 3 — Take your time. Consider: Do some items jump out as most important, regardless of where they appear? Do some further down the list surprise you? Note anything you haven't included — but keep working with what you have first.

STEP 4 — Identify any words that mean the same thing to you — not in a dictionary sense, but in terms of how you actually express them in your life. If so, combine them. If they are expressed differently, keep both.

STEP 5 — Keep repeating Step 4 until you have identified your THREE KEY VALUES: the ones that feel too important right now to ignore.

These three values are yours to sit with for the next 48 hours. Try keeping one at the top of your thinking for every decision you make. Consider how your actions — your doing — line up with this value. Ask yourself: What does this value mean to me, and how do I express it in my life?

WHOSE VALUES ARE YOU LIVING?

Writing a list of values is all very well. Understanding what you do each and every day to express those values — that is where the revelations live.

The reality is, we don't always know what we truly value. And sometimes what we believe we value is actually someone else's value — absorbed from family, culture, workplace, or the expectations of those around us.

There is a useful distinction between espoused values (what we say we value) and actual values (what our behaviour reveals that we value). They are not always the same thing.

In April 2018, all hell broke loose over a game of cricket in Australia. Cricket is the national sport and is known as the Gentleman's Game, traditionally associated with values such as honour, integrity, collaboration, and pride — all wrapped up in the iconic Baggy Green cap. Astonishingly, during an International Test match between Australia and South Africa, the leadership group decided to employ a strategy known as ball tampering in order to gain an advantage. They decided to cheat.

Much outrage followed when they were caught. Without litigating the pros and cons of their behaviour, it is a perfect example of espoused values (honour, integrity) versus actual values (winning — at all costs). It is also an example of how we are influenced by those around us to engage in behaviour that may conflict with our own value system.

We are human. We live, we learn, and we mostly get opportunities to be better. The purpose of the following exercise is not to judge yourself — it is to see clearly. You cannot navigate by a map you have never looked at.

EXERCISE TWO: Values Alignment Check

This exercise helps you track whether you are genuinely living your values — or living someone else's.

STEP 1 — Consider an activity, decision, or behaviour you engaged in over the past three days.

STEP 2 — Ask yourself: What values does this activity or choice express?

STEP 3 — Does this align with the three key values you identified in Exercise One?

For any decisions or choices where there is a mismatch — where behaviour and value point in different directions — notice how you feel when you look at it honestly. A twinge of guilt, frustration, resentment, or confusion often signals that your values are being overridden.

Ask yourself: Am I the one ignoring my own values? Am I being influenced by others — adopting their values as my own? Is there a fear of being left out, or of disappointing someone, that is driving me to compromise what is important to me?

This is not designed to send you into self-criticism. It is designed to return you to the driver's seat. Your authentic self will be found in the place where your values and your behaviours align. The more they separate, the more discomfort and dis-ease you will feel. The more they align, the more you will feel the quiet power of living from your Legacy Space.

EXERCISE THREE: Your Legacy Statement

This is a single sentence. It is not meant to be perfect. It is meant to be honest.

Complete this sentence:

"I want to be remembered for ______________________, because I value ______________________."

Examples:

"I want to be remembered for creating a safe space in my community, because I value belonging and courage."

"I want to be remembered for raising children who are kind, because I value love and integrity."

"I want to be remembered for the art I created, because I value freedom of expression."

"I want to be remembered for showing up, because I value connection."

There is no wrong answer. There is only your answer. Write it. Hold it. Let it guide you.

PART FOUR

WOMEN WHO DID IT

The Six 'C' Archetypes

> "Our deepest fear is not that we are inadequate. Our deepest fear is that we are powerful beyond measure. It is our light, not our darkness that most frightens us."
>
> Marianne Williamson

What happens when you think of leaving a legacy? Do you feel those bubbles of self-doubt, inadequacy, and fear pop to the surface? Do you believe that perhaps legacy belongs only to the legends — those with something unique to offer? Are you frightened by your own power?

You are not alone. And in this moment, you are in very good company.

This section is about women who lived their values — often regardless of reward or recognition — and by doing so created a legacy. In some cases, they became iconic. In others, they remain quietly extraordinary. In each, you will be able to see how doing what you love, and living what you value, can bring more power to you and let your light shine.

In examining how they lived their values, we can get a glimpse of how legacy expands outward from who we are being and what we are doing. We can also see how our focus values — the ones we consistently return to — become our super power: the strength guiding us through adversity and change.

A SELF-ASSESSMENT BEFORE YOU BEGIN

The six archetypes that follow are Culturists, Conservationists, Champions, Creators, Compassionists, and Connectors. You might connect with one — or you might find yourself in all six.

To help you begin, consider these questions before reading on:

> Where do you find yourself most energised?
>
> What area of life do you return to again and again, even when it is not convenient?
>
> When do you lose track of time?

Use these as a compass as you explore each archetype. Pay attention to which one — or which combination — makes something click.

CULTURISTS

One engaged in a culture. An advocate of culture or of a particular method of cultivating mind or body.

A Culturist might be an artist of any mode — film, music, cooking, painting — equally as well as a yogi, a student or teacher of theology or religion, anyone engaged in anthropology. Culture is the collective of who we are as individuals. Our collective beliefs, concepts of self, ideas of hierarchy, and judgements of right and wrong all add to the melting pot. Among us are people who are able to reflect back to us the best and worst of what our culture is being, and challenge our ideas. These people have an internal sense of self they are prepared to share with the many.

Frida Kahlo

The exhibition of Frida Kahlo's work that now travels the world guides visitors through a confronting journey: the life of a woman who not only painted herself but defined herself. Frida's life was short — she died at forty-seven — and tumultuous. She expressed herself with a raw honesty that remains startling.

She painted everything about the experience of being a woman: the feeling of strangeness, of being flawed, of beauty, of birth, miscarriage, and sexuality. Frida was both masculine and feminine, easily recognised by her trademark unibrow; her paintings are full of colour and of trauma in equal measure. Inextricably connected with the influences of Mexico and the post-revolutionary society she grew up in, her work exuded a narrative of a search for self, and an understanding of beauty in its rawest form.

Frida endured a tense marriage and lived in a period where women were gaining in status but were still viewed largely as property. And yet she unashamedly expressed herself and persisted in her discovery of self through priority values of Freedom, Tolerance, Culture, Beauty, and Meaning.

She was the first Mexican artist to be featured on a US postage stamp. When feminism took hold in the decades following her death, Kahlo was heralded as an icon for the movement and for female creativity. Her bold expression of femininity — as an artist and multi-faceted woman — continues to move people. But her most enduring legacy may be this: permission to be wholly yourself, in all your contradiction and complexity.

Marilyn Monroe

Marilyn Monroe may seem a contradiction to Frida Kahlo, but the similarities in their internal struggle for self are striking. Marilyn became an iconic symbol of beauty and fashion which endures today. But what were her defining values?

Art and Beauty were both highly valued by Marilyn. Post-1955 she refused to be cast as a "dumb blonde" and expressed fierce determination to be taken seriously. Marilyn was fiercely intelligent and began her own production company. She is reported to have said: "I am a serious actress, I want to be taken seriously."

Marilyn's search for self, as with Frida's, is peppered across her life story and her tragic demise. Both women overcame pain — emotional and physical — born from the experience of abuse, and in each you can see the expression of the value of Search and Meaning.

The tragedy of Marilyn Monroe's life is not only its ending. It is that she may never have been fully seen. Her legacy, like Frida's, lives in the permission her existence grants others: to want more, to want to be taken seriously, to refuse to be reduced to someone else's expectation.

* * *

CONSERVATIONISTS

One who advocates for the preservation of the natural world.

A Conservationist is someone whose area of influence is the living world — who sees connection and beauty in nature and who dedicates their energy to preservation and protection. These are women whose legacy extends across generations, whose work will matter long after they are gone.

Dian Fossey

Dian Fossey's work with mountain gorillas in Rwanda is among the most remarkable acts of conservation of the twentieth century. Fossey devoted her life to the study and protection of the gorillas of the Virunga Mountains. Her research was groundbreaking. Her commitment was absolute. Her courage was extraordinary.

Fossey arrived in Africa in 1966 with no background in primatology. She had a background in occupational therapy and a profound love of animals. She taught herself field research, learned the gorillas' behaviours, and ultimately habituated them to human presence in ways that enabled her to study them at close range. Her findings changed the world's understanding of the great apes.

She was murdered in 1985, almost certainly by those with an interest in poaching. Her death did not end her legacy — it amplified it. Her book Gorillas in the Mist and the subsequent film brought global attention to the plight of the mountain gorilla. The Dian Fossey Gorilla Fund International continues her work today.

Fossey's values are visible in every aspect of her life: Passion, Commitment, Conservation, Courage, and Service. She did not seek fame. She sought the gorillas. And in finding them, she changed everything.

Terri Irwin

Terri Irwin continues the legacy of her late husband Steve — and in doing so has built a formidable legacy of her own. Through the Australia Zoo and the conservation work it supports, Terri has maintained and expanded the Irwin family's commitment to wildlife while also raising two extraordinary children in the same spirit.

What is remarkable about Terri's legacy is not simply what she has preserved, but how she has built it: with grace, with quiet determination, and with a values system that prioritises the living world above almost everything else. Following profound personal loss, she chose intention over accident. She chose the legacy she wanted to leave and has been building it every day since.

★ ★ ★

CHAMPIONS

One who fights for a cause or on behalf of another person.

A Champion is someone who takes up the fight — for themselves, for others, for an idea. Champions are not necessarily famous. They are not always loud. They are persistent in the face of resistance, and they know what they are fighting for.

Serena Williams

It is difficult to summarise the legacy of Serena Williams in a few paragraphs. Her record speaks for itself: twenty-three Grand Slam singles titles, four Olympic gold medals, a career spanning more than two decades of sustained excellence.

But her legacy extends beyond sport. Serena has been a Champion in the truest sense — of herself, of women in sport, of Black women in a sport that was not built for them, of mothers who refused to be diminished by motherhood. She returned to the tennis court after giving birth to her daughter Olympia, having survived life-threatening complications. She has spoken openly about the challenges faced by Black women in healthcare, and has used her platform consistently and courageously.

Serena's values — Excellence, Courage, Justice, Family, and Resilience — have shaped not just her own career but the culture of sport itself. She has changed what is possible for every young girl who picks up a racquet and dares to imagine herself the greatest.

Ordinary Champions

The Champion archetype is not reserved for Olympians and Grand Slam winners. It lives in every woman who refuses to shrink, who persists when it would be easier to stop, who uses what she has to fight for what she loves.

Consider:

> A primary school teacher who, after thirty years in the classroom, realises her legacy is not in the curriculum she taught but in the seventy students she mentored who became teachers themselves. She has spent her career building other people's confidence in the quiet, daily, unremarkable work of showing up. That is a Champion's legacy.

> A bookkeeper who spent decades managing the finances of her community rugby club, who in her retirement began recording the oral histories of the club's founding families. No one asked her to do it. She did it because she valued history, community, and the stories of ordinary people. The archive she created is now housed at the local library. She is a Champion.
>
> A woman who, following her own recovery from illness, started a running group for women over forty who had never run before. She had no experience as a coach — only conviction, values around community and health, and the knowledge of what it felt like to start from nothing. A decade later, her group has branches in three cities. She is a Champion.

None of these women set out to build a legacy. They set out to do the thing that felt most true to who they were. That is exactly how an intentional legacy is built.

We all have a personal story — the narrative of our lives, the trauma we are overcoming, the accomplishments, the service, and the joys. However big or small we see them, they play a role in forging our legacy. Our challenge, our hero quest, the Champion in each of us, has the opportunity to take a look at what those pieces are — and there is no need for super powers.

CREATORS

One that creates, usually by bringing something new or original into being.

Not wanting to tread on anyone's faith in identifying a theme of Creator, I suggest we can all find a little of ourselves here. Creating a legacy comes from sometimes very small sparks of talent and attention. There is no one who cannot leave a lasting legacy.

Trelise Cooper

New Zealand designer Trelise Cooper is warm, attentive, and sparkling. As she has reflected on her journey from early days through to international success, her values are clearly articulated in her own words: "I like that I'm untrained because it gives me freedom of expression."

So many of us get caught up on our lack of training, education, or qualification — and here Trelise embraces being her authentic self and the freedom of being untrained. Rather than feeling limited through lack of training, Trelise feels unlimited. Simply wonderful.

Trelise also expresses how she values Meditation and Contemplation — how taking time to explore self and environment informs her creative self. Courage too is reflected in her recollection of the fear she feels for every fashion show. Putting oneself out into any field opens the door to criticism and judgement. Courage, as the saying goes, is not the absence of fear, but action in the face of it.

Coco Chanel

Gabrielle Bonheur "Coco" Chanel clearly valued Freedom and Courage above almost everything else. Separating freedom, expression of self, and creativity in her work would be difficult — they are so thoroughly interwoven.

Chanel seemed compelled by a burning need to express herself. She was a rule-breaker who saw the constraints experienced by women in what they wore as unacceptable. Her designs were at the forefront of a revolution in women's wear — created with liberation and freedom in mind. The introduction of the Chanel Suit post-World War II incorporated traditional men's design into everyday wear for women who were populating the workforce in numbers never previously seen.

The death of her mother resulted in Coco and her sisters being raised in a

Catholic orphanage where she learned to sew. She drew on that skill and on her values throughout her entire life, creating her world on her own terms. She expressed her understanding of courage in a sentence that rings as true today as it ever did: "The most courageous act is still to think for yourself. Aloud."

Maya Angelou

Maya Angelou fits in equal measure into the realm of Culturist and Creator. Her legacy in culture was produced through her priority values of Freedom of Expression and — above all — Courage. "Without courage," she wrote, "we cannot practise any other virtue with consistency. We can't be kind, true, merciful, generous, or honest."

Her practice of working from the space of her values increased her area of influence until it rippled across a culture and across time. Angelou's search for self is woven through all her work: "When I'm writing, I am trying to find out who I am, who we are, what we're capable of, how we feel, how we lose and stand up, and go on from darkness into darkness."

That is a Legacy Statement, hidden in plain sight.

★ ★ ★

COMPASSIONISTS

Having or showing compassion. Dedicated to the wellbeing of others.

There is no single word for someone who dedicates their life to creating a legacy whereby others are inspired to reach out and engage in activities for the greater good. Into the realm of Compassionist I include all the carers, teachers, nurses, emergency services workers, and those engaged in community clubs and enterprises. You will know them in your community — the ones running the barbecue so the local kids can have a new playground, the ones organising meals for a family when there is a fellow woman fighting cancer even though they have a full-time job and a family of their own to feed.

Mother Teresa and Angelina Jolie

In choosing Mother Teresa and Angelina Jolie, I have selected two women with common values and deeply different life experiences — perhaps even the sinner and the saint, though who is which may depend on your own values.

In each woman you can see the expression of Care, Nurture, and Service. Mother Teresa's values were expressed throughout her entire life; Angelina Jolie discovered the fullest expression of hers later, in her work as a UN Goodwill Ambassador and in her advocacy for those affected by conflict and displacement.

Imagine these two women in conversation, sharing their stories of reaching out, extending care, honouring the individual, and raising awareness. They are two women with shared desires and goals who would support each other's mission freely and openly. It is this type of conversation that breaks down barriers and finds areas of commonality where collaboration and conviction can create change.

Katharine Hepburn

Katharine Hepburn may not seem an obvious Compassionist, but look more closely.

Throughout her career Hepburn used her platform to advocate for those without power, particularly women. She was among the first Hollywood stars to insist on wearing trousers — not as a fashion statement, but because she found them practical and refused to be governed by convention. When her clothing was repeatedly removed from her dressing room by studio employees who objected, she simply appeared on set without anything else to wear until her trousers were returned.

She refused long-term contracts with studios that sought to control her choices. She produced her own work. She chose her collaborators with care and maintained lifelong relationships of genuine depth and equality.

Hepburn was not a saint. She was an independent woman who valued Freedom, Integrity, Courage, and Authenticity — and who expressed those values through everything she did with an uncommon consistency. She was authentic even when authenticity cost her professionally. She operated from her values even when it ruffled feathers.

Her legacy is not simply the films. It is the permission her way of living granted to every woman who saw in her a different kind of possibility: that you could refuse to be what others needed you to be, and build something extraordinary from the refusal.

★ ★ ★

CONNECTORS

One who creates connection between people, ideas, and communities.

Connection plays a vital role in our daily lives. We network, we keep in touch, we reach out. We are social beings, wired for connection — and among us are those whose particular gift, whose particular value, is the ability to connect others with each other, with ideas, with themselves.

Just as we all have a little of each of the archetypes in us, we are all Connectors. The most important connection you will make, however, will be with yourself.

Oprah Winfrey

It is hard to imagine there was a time in her adult life when Oprah Winfrey did not know what she wanted. And yet there was. More aptly — and exactly as this book encourages you to do — Oprah had a moment when she realised she had to ask herself: What do I really want?

Her answer: "What I really want is to connect."

From humble beginnings and an extraordinarily difficult early life, Oprah built a career on this single value. Her childhood story and the abuse she suffered are well known. She developed a powerful desire for safety and survival, utilising her extraordinary skill in communication to create security. As her confidence grew, her values appear to have expanded from self-preservation to social justice, inclusion, and — above all — connection.

As her skills and confidence increased, her passion and influence grew. The combination created the opportunity to connect with others and help them connect with their own personal values, their authentic selves. Oprah's legacy began to manifest. From humble beginnings, with perseverance and the courage to look within, she is living a life that leaves a legacy. With no super powers required.

WHAT'S NEXT?

> Life is either a daring adventure or nothing at all.
> Helen Keller

Take one thing, one value, and pursue it with passion. It might be the most unbalanced act you have ever engaged in.

Ask yourself each day: What do I want to be remembered for? Who do I want to be remembered as? Let your mind do the work. Let the pathways and opportunities open up. Take action in line with the answers. If you are nudged to go for a walk, to reach out to someone, to start something small — do it.

Stay in your legacy space when you connect with others. Ask them what is important to them and listen to what they say. Hear what they value. See how you can connect. Observe for yourself who you are being.

This isn't a test. There is no pass or fail. You cannot look at someone else to get the answers. Your answers will be unique to you.

This is much more than reaching a goal or ticking something off a bucket list. This is about how you travel this adventure of your life. Choose a value — one value. It won't mean your other values are neglected; it might actually result in all your values becoming satisfied. Choose a value that might deliver what you really want. Find a way to express it — do it in service to others, use your talents, your skills, your knowledge. Bring your value alive.

Ask yourself the tough questions, and be patient enough to give your mind — and the universe — a chance to answer.

If you value leadership, consider what your leadership legacy might be. Observe the answers in the behaviours around you. Who are you being in the workplace, in the community, at home? Are you being a leader you would want to follow?

If you value family, ask yourself the tough questions about how you show up in family life. Can you be brave enough to let go? To trust in love and in your higher self?

It might feel unbalanced and uncomfortable to begin with. It might shift everything. It might create a whole new you. It will bring you into service of others. It might bring new relationships and new adventures. Find a mentor. Find a coach. Find a friend. Share with them what you plan to focus on.

★ ★ ★

On a final note, consider this: legacies are not built only by those in the spotlight. They are built in the ordinary moments of an ordinary life, by people who know what they value and who choose — again and again — to express it.

A woman named Sara was diagnosed with a serious illness in her early thirties. During her treatment she discovered a talent for crochet. She began making blankets — handcrafted, beautifully coloured, made with the finest materials she could find. Each one a labour of quiet focus. When she had too many for her own home, she began donating them to the neonatal intensive care unit at her local hospital, where tiny babies would be wrapped in something made with care, attention, and love. Families have called them heirlooms. Sara will tell you she didn't set out to create a legacy. She set out to do something with her hands while her body healed.

That is exactly how an intentional legacy often begins — with one small act, in line with one deep value, done with consistency and love.

Where will your legacy start? And where will it take you?

★ ★ ★

> "Life will break you. Nobody can protect you from that, and living alone won't either, for solitude will also break you with its yearning. You have to love. You have to feel. It is the reason you are here on earth. You are here to risk your heart. You are here to be swallowed up. And when it happens that you are broken, or betrayed, or left or hurt, or death brushes near, let yourself sit by an apple tree and listen to the apples falling all around you in heaps, wasting their sweetness. Tell yourself you tasted as many as you could."

Louise Erdrich, The Painted Drum

NOTES & SOURCES

PART TWO: WHY LEGACY MATTERS

Annie's story is drawn from public court records and newspaper archives. The inquest proceedings were published in The Star, Christchurch, New Zealand, February 1888.

Statistics on domestic violence reporting: Keys Young (1998). Against the Odds: How Women Survive Domestic Violence. Australian Bureau of Statistics (1996). Women's Safety Australia.

Leah Warshawski TEDx talk: How Do You Cope with the Trauma You Didn't Experience. TEDx Twin Falls. Available at https://youtu.be/OkAMHQhabkU

Herero genocide and the New York Museum: Gross, D.A. The Troubling Origins of the Skeletons in a New York Museum. The New Yorker. https://www.newyorker.com/culture/culture-desk/the-troubling-origins-of-the-skeletons-in-a-new-york-museum

Epigenetics — environmental memory transmission: Phys.org (2017). Environmental Memories. https://phys.org/news/2017-04-environmental-memories.html

Nature Neuroscience study on transgenerational epigenetic inheritance reported by BBC Health (2013). https://www.bbc.com/news/health-25156510. Full study: Nature Neuroscience 17, 89–96 (2014). https://www.nature.com/articles/nn.3594

PART FOUR: WOMEN WHO DID IT

Frida Kahlo — feminist icon and legacy: leader-values.com. https://www.leader-values.com/leader.php?lid=127

Marilyn Monroe: Vanity Fair profile (2010). https://www.vanityfair.com/culture/2010/11/marilyn-monroe-201011

Dian Fossey: Dian Fossey Gorilla Fund International. https://gorillafund.org/who-we-are/dian-fossey/

Serena Williams on raising her daughter: Us Magazine. https://www.usmagazine.com/celebrity-news/news/serena-williams-teaches-daughter-alexis-the-value-in-sports/

Oprah Winfrey interview with Jeff Weiner, LinkedIn Influencers, November 2017. https://www.slideshare.net/LinkedInPulse/oprah-winfrey-jeff-weiner-belief-leadership-career-intention

Trelise Cooper: I Know This To Be True [Salizzo, Blackwell, Chun. Published by PQ Blackwell Limited, 2016]

www.ingramcontent.com/pod-product-compliance
Lightning Source LLC
LaVergne TN
LVHW081302100826
845148LV00005B/945